Mad 4 Maths
6th Class

Len and Anne Frobisher

Carroll Education Limited

© Len and Anne Frobisher 2002
Under Licence from Pearson Education Limited
Original title published as Maths Plus Word Problems

This book is copyright and reproduction of the whole or part without the Publisher's written permission is prohibited.

This edition published in 2009 by Carroll Education Limited
34A Lavery Avenue
Park West Industrial Estate
Nangor Road
Dublin 12
http://www.carrolleducation.ie

Designers: DP Press Ltd, Sevenoaks, Kent and M & J Graphics, Harold's Cross, Dublin

Illustrators: Andy Hammond and Nicola Sedgwick

Cover Illustrator: Andrew Hunt

ISBN: 978-1-84450-148-9

All rights reserved. No part of this publication may be reproduced, stored in a retrieval system, or transmitted in any form or by any means, electronic, mechanical, photocopying, recording or otherwise, without either the prior permission of the Publisher or a licence permitting restricted copying in Ireland issued by the Irish Copyright Licensing Agency, 25 Denzille Lane, Dublin 2.

Contents

UNIT	TOPIC	PAGE

Autumn 1st half term

1. Number problems 1 4
2. Money problems 1 5
3. Number problems 2 6
4. Number problems 3 7
5. Number problems 4 8
6. Number problems 5 9
7. Review problems 1 10

Autumn 2nd half term

8. Measures problems 1 12
9. Length problems 1 13
10. Time problems 1 14
11. Money problems 2 15
12. Number problems 6 16
13. Number problems 7 17
14. Review problems 2 18

Spring 1st half term

1. Number problems 8 20
2. Money problems 3 21
3. Number problems 9 22
4. Number problems 10 23
5. Measures problems 2 24
6. Review problems 3 25

Spring 2nd half term

7. Weight problems 1 26
8. Measures problems 3 27
9. Money problems 4 28
10. Number problems 11 29
11. Number problems 12 30
12. Number problems 13 31
13. Review problems 4 32

Summer 1st half term

1. Number problems 14 34
2. Money problems 5 35
3. Number problems 15 36
4. Number problems 16 37
5. Number problems 17 38
6. Number problems 18 39
7. Review problems 5 40

Summer 2nd half term

8. Capacity problems 1 42
9. Measures problems 4 43
10. Numbers problems 19 44
11. Money problems 6 45
12. Number problems 20 46
13. Number problems 21 47
14. Review problems 6 48

Number problems 1

1 In a golf tournament Julie has rounds of 86 and 95.

What is Julie's total score? 181

2 In a gymnastics competition a team has ten members. They each score 8.9 points.

What is the total points score of the team? 89

3 A machine makes 37 000 candles each day and packs them into boxes of 100.

How many boxes are packed each day? 370

4 A car park has 63 parking places. There are 47 cars in the car park.

How many empty places are there? 18

5 Ten judges give a total score of 45 in an ice-skating competition. Each judge awards the same score.

What score did each judge award? 4.5

6 There are 100 paper clips in a box and 100 boxes in a carton.

How many paper clips are in one carton? 10 000

7  Divide me by 10 and multiply the answer by 100. You will get 32. 0.32 What am I?

Money problems 1

1 Mr O'Brien buys a car for himself for €5900 and another for his wife for €3800. What is the total cost of the two cars?

€8,700

2 A newsagent sells 25 copies of a magazine. Each copy is €3.60. What is the total amount of money that the newsagent receives?

€80

3.60
× 25

1800
6200

3 Mr and Mrs Butler book a round the world holiday. The total cost is €9200. They pay a deposit of €1700. How much is left for them to pay?

€7,500

4 The normal price for a TV is €500. In the sale it is reduced by 25%. By how much is the TV reduced?

€375

5 Jack's mum buys a microwave for €84.90 and a vacuum cleaner for €37.50 from a catalogue. How much does she pay when she collects them?

€122.40

84.90
+37.50

122.40

6 Mr Grey buys 25 swing ball sets to sell in his shop. He pays a total of €440. How much does he pay for each swing ball set?

25)440
−25↓

7

*I am between €6 and €9.
I am a multiple of 50c.
I divide exactly by 2 and by 3.*

What am I?

€6

Number problems 2

1. Helen wants 42 balloons for a party. Each packet has 6 balloons.

How many packets does she need to buy?

2. In two high board dives Seán was awarded a total of 10 points. In his first dive Adam scored 5.2 points.

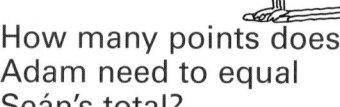

How many points does Adam need to equal Seán's total?

3. Arklow's football ground has a capacity of 7495 spectators. In six successive home games Arklow play in front of a full ground.

What is the total number of spectators who watch the six games?

4. Mrs O'Brien counts 33 children on to a bus for a school trip. There are 76 more still to come.

How many children are going on the school trip?

5. Mr Evans, a baker, makes 72 muffins. He puts them on trays, 8 muffins to each tray.

How many trays does he use?

6. In an ISPCA kennels there are 82 stray dogs. Shortly after Christmas another 18 strays are brought in.

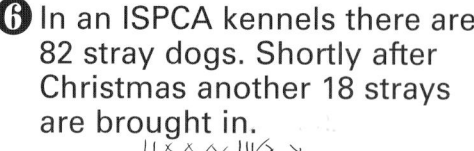

How many stray dogs are in the kennels then?

7.

*I am a square number.
I am less than 80.
I am a multiple of 9.*

What am I?

Number problems 3

1 There are 850 passengers waiting for trains. Another 150 join them.
What is the total number waiting for trains?

2 An airport has seven stands for planes. Each stand can take eight planes.
What is the total number of planes on the stands when they are all full?

3 A pizza parlour makes ten pizzas. Each pizza is cut into six pieces. They sell three whole pizzas and 5 single pieces.

How many pizzas are left as a mixed number?

4 In every pack there are six packets of crisps. Each packet weighs 25 g. Fiona buys eight packs for a party.

How many packets of crisps does Fiona buy?

5 On the first day of a two-day Steam Fair 350 balloons are launched in a distance competition. On the second day another 650 are let go.
Altogether how many balloons are launched?

6 A cafe makes six apple pies. Each apple pie is cut into eighths. The cafe sells $4\frac{3}{4}$ pies.
How many eighths are left?

7  *I am a square number. I am the sum of three odd numbers between 20 and 30.* What am I?

Number problems 4

1 At Glennvara Primary School 3 in every 5 children are girls.

What percentage of the children are girls?

2 There are 15 people in an adult swimming lesson. For every 2 men there are 3 women.

How many are men?
How many are women?

3 Monaghan GAA football club has won 50% of their 20 matches and drawn 10%.

How many matches has Monaghan lost?

4 A box contains 20 golf balls. One in every five balls are found to be faulty.

How many golf balls in the box are faulty?

5 Three-tenths of a case of oranges are thrown away as they are bad.

What percentage of the oranges are OK?

6 A maths test had 20 questions. Aoife got 85% correct.

How many questions did Aoife get wrong?

7

I have three factors. The sum of my factors is 7.

What am I?

Number problems 5

1 A car transporter with a trailer always carries 14 cars. In two years it makes 1000 deliveries. How many cars does it deliver in the two years?

2 Tim plays a game of 'Score 4 or more' with Andrew. They take turns to throw a six-sided dice. A point is awarded if they roll 4 or more. What is the probability that Tim will score a point when he rolls the dice?

3 Holly keeps fish. She has seven large tanks. In each tank there are 28 fish. Altogether how many fish does Holly have?

4 Robert tosses a fair coin five times. Each time it lands 'head'. What is the probability that next time he tosses the coin it will land 'head'?

5 A school has seven classes. Two classes have 27 children, two classes have 30 children and three classes have 25 children. What is the range of the number of children in the seven classes?

6 In one day a machine produces 137 000 vitamin tablets and puts them in jars of 1000. How many jars does it fill in the one day?

7  I am more than 70. I am the sum of three consecutive numbers. The difference between my two digits is 3. What am I?

Review problems 1

1. Mr and Mrs O'Reilly took their family, Emma (17), Liam (14), Siobhán (12) and the children's grandmother (63) and grandfather (62) to London during the summer holidays, where they rode on the London Eye. They had booked their tickets for the ride two weeks before they went.
What was the total cost for the seven of them?

2. How much would the O'Reilly family have saved had they gone in May instead of the summer holidays?

3. The O'Reilly family travelled from Dublin by ferry and train. They got the 07:30 train which was due to arrive in King's Cross, London at 10:50. It arrived 17 minutes late.
How long did the journey take?

4. The London Eye operates every day of the year.
What is the total number of hours it is operating in one year?

5. How many people are on the London Eye when it is full?

6. A ride on the Eye takes a gently paced half an hour. The ride moves at the same speed and never stops moving until it closes at the end of the day.
How many full turns did it make on 15th September?

7. There is a metal rope from the centre of the Eye to each capsule. What is the angle between each rope?

8. The average weight of a man is 73.5 kg and a woman 61.3 kg. What is the approximate total weight in a capsule which contains 10 men and 10 women?

9. The Eye is 135 metres high. A double-decker bus is 5 metres high. How many times higher is the Eye than a double-decker bus?

10. It is predicted that 2 million visitors will ride on the Eye every year for the next five years. If the actual number is only 90% of the prediction how many will ride on the Eye in the next five years?

Measures problems 1

1. Adam tried to triple jump for the first time. He hopped 2.7 m, stepped 1.8 m and jumped 2.9 metres.

How long was his triple jump?

2. An average 10-year-old boy weighs 36 kg. This is 10 times the average weight of a newly born boy.

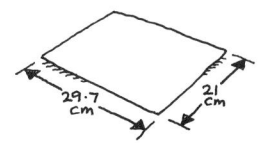

What is the average weight of a newly born boy?

3. An A4 sheet of paper is 21 cm wide and 29.7 cm long.

What is the perimeter of a piece of A4 paper?

4. Amy buys an electric radiator. It is 25 cm tall and 60 cm wide.

What is the total surface area of the radiator?

5. Ciara opens a full bottle of 2.5 litres of lemonade. She pours out two glasses with 200 mL in each glass.

How much lemonade is left in the bottle?

6. Steve flies from Dublin to Sydney. The total time for the journey was 45 hours. The plane stops at three airports to refuel for a total of 17 hours.

For how long was Steve actually flying?

7.  *I am the sum of four consecutive numbers. The four numbers are between 16 and 23. The first and last numbers are multiples of 3.* What am I?

Length problems 1

1) In 1991 the world record for the long jump, set by Mike Powell, was 8.95 m. A fully sized python is 20% longer than this.
How long is a fully sized python?

2) In 1930 a man dived into the sea using only air to a depth of 105 m. Thirty years later a man in a bathyscaphe went to 100 times this depth.
How many kilometres deep did the bathyscaphe go?

3) The longest Olympic event is the 50 km road walk.

What is the length of the walk in metres?

4) In the year 2000 the women's javelin record was 67.09 m. The men's record was 98.48 m.
How much longer was the men's than the women's record distance?

5) The distance from Paris, France to Rome, Italy is 1098 km. The distance from New York, USA to Beijing, China is 10 times this.

How far is it from New York to Beijing?

6) The tallest building in the world used to be the Empire State Building in New York at 381 m. In 2001 the tallest was the CN Tower in Toronto. It is 128 m higher than the Empire State Building.

What is the height of the CN Tower?

7)  *I have only two factors. The difference between the two factors is 16.* What am I?

Time problems 1

1 When people are eating breakfast in New York at 8 a.m. Dubliners are having lunch at 1 p.m.

What is the time difference between New York and Dublin?

2 Mary has a seconds watch. Her brother runs on the spot for 750 seconds and jumps up and down for 250 seconds.

What is the total time on Mary's watch in minutes and seconds?

3 The time in Mexico City is 8 hours behind the time in Limerick.

What day and time is it in Mexico City when it is 3 a.m. on a Tuesday in Limerick?

4 Michael breathes in and out in 1.9 seconds.

How many seconds will it take him to breathe in and out 100 times?

5 Niamh measures her pulse rate. She finds that her pulse beats 100 times in 90 seconds.

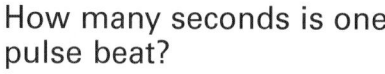

How many seconds is one pulse beat?

6 Tokyo in Japan is 9 hours ahead of the time in Belfast. It is 08:00 on a Sunday in Tokyo.

What day and time is it in Belfast?

7  I am the sum of five consecutive numbers. The middle of the five numbers is 15. What am I?

Money problems 2

1 Louise posts a letter and a parcel. The letter costs her €0.85 and the parcel double the cost of the letter.

How much does the parcel cost Louise?

2 Chloe's mum and dad buy the table and four chairs, and the cupboard.

What is the total cost of the table, chairs and cupboard?

3 The normal price of a car is €12 000. Ben's dad gets a discount of €1200.

What is the percentage discount that Ben's dad gets?

4 Tara goes with her friends for a party meal at Billy Burgers. It costs her dad €51 for the ten of them.

What is the average cost for each person?

5 Katie's mum withdraws €500 from the bank. She spends €397 of it on a short holiday for the family.

How much of the €500 is left?

6 The pre-sale price for a camcorder is €650. It is reduced in the sale by 20%.

What is the price of the camcorder in the sale?

7  *I am only divisible by 1 and 37.* What am I?

Number problems 6

1 A company employs 3841 workers. It merges with another company that has 1996 employees to form a new company.

How many people are employed by the merged new company?

2 Aisling takes part in a gymnastics competition. In her first attempt on the beam she falls and only scores 4.6 points. She scores double this on her second attempt.

How many does Aisling score on her second attempt?

3 At the Autumn Fair Fiona sells cakes. She displays eight plates with eight tarts on each plate.

Altogether how many tarts are on the plates?

4 The attendance at Meath Ladies first football match was 1741. The attendance at the next game increased to 2219.

What was the increase in attendance?

5 A local council owns houses and flats. There are 8608 people living in houses and 4295 in flats.

What is the total number of people living in houses and flats?

6 Thomond Park Stadium has room for 26 500 spectators. There are 15 100 seats.

How many spectators stand when the ground is full?

7  My greatest factor is 64. What am I?

Number problems 7

1. Jumpers are boxed in sixes. Mr Daly takes delivery of 43 boxes for his shop. How many jumpers have been delivered to his shop?

2. In a competition there are 180 hot air balloons. One hour after the time to take off one-tenth of them are still on the ground.
How many are still on the ground?

3. The cost of a packet of Wheatcrunch is €1.25. The number in a packet is increased from 24 to 36 without an increase in the price.
What is the percentage increase in the number of Wheatcrunches in a box?

4. In an hour, a machine makes 300 000 chocolate drops and puts them into packets of 100.

How many packets are produced in one hour?

5. In a dance competition Jodie and Ryan score 4.4 points in the Jive and 5.6 points in the Disco.
What is their total score after the two dances?

6. Medallions are made of famous athletes to celebrate the Olympic Games. A machine makes 1 million every day. They are packed in boxes of 1000.
How many boxes are packed every day?

7. *The sum of my four prime factors is 17.* What am I?

Review problems 2

1. Mr and Mrs Dolan live between Knock and Sligo. They want to take their three children to Lapland.
How much will it cost them to go from Sligo?
How much cheaper would it be for them to go from Knock?

2. It takes the Dolan family 1 hr 15 min to get to Knock Airport. They should arrive 2 hours before the 07:05 flight.
At what time should they leave home?

3. At what time is the 07:05 flight from Knock due to land in Lapland?

4. The distance from Mr and Mrs Dolan's home to Knock airport is 80 km. From Knock to Santa's Village is 2370 km.
How far will the Dolan family have travelled when they arrive home?

5. When the Dolan family travel there are 3 children in every 5 people on board the plane. Altogether there are 135 passengers.
How many children are on the plane?

6. On the flight from Belfast there are 58 adults and 97 children, and 10 crew. What is the total number of people on the plane?

7. Altogether a total of 1251 people travel to Lapland on the advertised flights.
What is the average number of passengers per airport?

8. When they arrive in Lapland Mr Dolan and two of the children go on a snowmobile and the whole family go on a reindeer sleigh ride. Altogether how much does it cost them?

9. There are ten sleighs each pulled by eight huskies at the Santa Claus Village. How many huskies are there altogether?

10. On the Sligo trip 79 people wish to go on a reindeer ride. How many journeys will the sleighs make?

11. A large group of 36 children and 20 adults book from Shannon. They get a reduction of 15% off the total cost.
How much does the group pay?

12. Plan and cost a visit to Lapland for your family.

Number problems 8

1. Jamie and his friends give out leaflets advertising a rock concert. On Monday they give out 6000, on Tuesday 8000 and on Wednesday 5000.

Altogether how many leaflets did they give out?

2. In the first hour of a sale 93 people enter a shop. Of these, 78 buy an item in the sale.

How many do not buy an item?

3. In South Dakota, USA, on 22nd January 1943 the temperature rose from −20°C to 7°C in two minutes.

By how many degrees did the temperature rise in the two minutes?

4. There were 7200 tickets sold for an open air concert. It rained heavily on the night and only 6700 people attended.

How many people with tickets did not attend the concert?

5. Fifth Class sell 72 tickets for a combined 5th Class and 6th Class disco. Sixth Class sell 89 tickets.

Altogether how many tickets do they sell?

6. At 11 p.m. the temperature at a school is −1°C. Seven hours later it has dropped by 4°C.

What is the temperature at 6 a.m?

7.  If you double me and subtract 1000 from the answer you get 4000. What am I?

Money problems 3

1 The normal price of the lawnmower is €600.
What is the sale price of the lawnmower?

2 For her 18th birthday Meghan's mum and dad buy her the ring and chain.
What is the total cost of the two items?

3 A china cup and saucer cost €7.60. Conor's mum buys eight cups and saucers.

What is the total cost of the eight cups and saucers?

4 Ben's aunt is getting married. His mum and dad spend €100 on two presents. They buy her the cutlery set.

How much do they spend on the kettle?

5 A pack of ten monster ice lollies costs €4.30.
What is the cost of one monster ice lolly?

6 Lucy's dad buys the motor car. He pays by credit card.
How much cash does he get back?

7  *I am a square number between 100 and 200. The sum of my first and last digits is 2 less than my middle digit.* What am I?

Number problems 9

1) A golf club has 500 members. Of these, 95% are adults.

How many members are children?

2) Five judges in a speaking competition each give Matthew 4.6 marks out of 5.

What is Matthew's total score?

3) Keith went on holiday for six days. He left lights on in the house and used 82.2 units of electricity.

How many units of electricity were used on each of the six days?

4) The earth's atmosphere is 78% nitrogen and 21% oxygen.

What percentage of the atmosphere is made up of other gases?

5) Ancient Egyptians made four mud bricks using a wooden frame.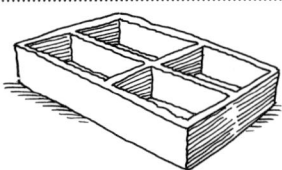

How many times would they have used the frame to make 748 bricks?

6) Anna throws three darts. She scores a total of 57. All three darts land in the same number.

What number did the darts land in?

7)  I am the smallest number that is divisible by 5, 6 and 9. What am I?

Number problems 10

1 A garden centre has 36 rose trees for sale. Another 48 rose trees are delivered and put out for sale. How many rose trees are for sale after the delivery?

2 A design in the floor of a Spanish house is made up of regular decagons, 10-sided polygons. Each angle is one-tenth of 1440°. How many degrees is each angle in a regular decagon?

3 A supermarket puts 95 Easter eggs on a shelf. They sell 58 of them within 30 minutes of opening.

How many Easter eggs are left on the shelf?

4 The ship carries 1000 cars. In one year the ship transports 8000 cars from Japan to Europe.

How many journeys does the ship make from Japan to Europe?

5 A publisher prints 3000 copies of a book. Two-fifths of the books have to be reprinted as they have pages missing.

How many books have to be reprinted?

6 In a funny faces competition Hannah scores 5.8 with her first funny face and 4.2 with her next.

How many did she score altogether?

7  *I am a two-digit number between 10 and 40. I am the sum of all my divisors.* What am I?

Measure problems 2

1 A spider in Papua New Guinea makes webs which are 1.5 m across.

How many centimetres across is a web?

2 The rhinoceros beetle is 19 cm long, including its horn. Its horn is one-half of its length.

How long is the horn of the rhinoceros beetle?

3 The track in a go-kart race is triangular. The triangle has angles of 60° and 85°.

What is the size of the third angle of the triangle?

4 Simon buys 0.7 kg of strawberries. He gives half of them to his brother.

How many grams of strawberries does Simon have left?

5 A three-toed sloth spends 0.75 of a day hanging upside down.

What fraction of a day does it spend the right way up?

6 A bottle of Jamult holds 65 ml. They are sold in packs of seven. They are delivered to supermarkets in crates of 1000 packs.

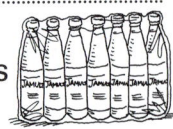

How many litres of Jamult are in each crate?

7  I am half-way between two consecutive numbers. The product of the two numbers is 650.

What am I?

Review problems 3

You may find it helpful to use a calculator.
You must show your workings.

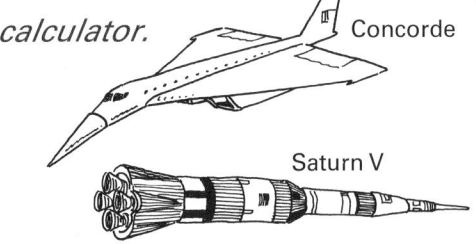

❶ Concorde carried 148 passengers and crew across the Atlantic from London to New York and back twice a day. If it had full capacity on each journey how many people did it carry in one week?

❷ The first powered flight was by Orville Wright in 1903. Concorde first flew in 1969.
How many years after Orville Wright's flight was this?

❸ The first air speed record was set by P. Tissandier in 1909 in a Wright Biplane at 34.03 m.p.h. Concorde flew at 1450 m.p.h. How many times faster was Concorde than the 1909 record to the nearest whole number?

❹ The official air speed record in 2001 was held by a MiG-25. It travelled at 1.455 times the speed of Concorde (1450 m.p.h.). What was the record in 2001 to the nearest whole number?

❺ In April 1990 Concorde travelled from New York to London in 2 hr 55 min. If it left New York at 19:00, when would it have arrived in London which is 5 hours ahead?

❻ The take-off weight of Concorde was 185 000 kg. The Saturn V rocket was 16 times as heavy as Concorde at take-off. What was the weight of the Saturn V rocket at take-off?

❼ Concorde had a wing span of 83.33 ft and a length of 203.75 ft.
What were its wing span and length in metres to the nearest hundredth? (1 ft = 0.3048 m)

Weight problems 1

1 If a new 50c coin weighs 15 grams, what is the weight of a bag of 50c coins that is worth €4.50?

2 A golf ball weighs 45 g. This is 30 times the weight of a pygmy shrew, the world's smallest mammal.

What is the weight of a pygmy shrew?

3 Emma weighs out 700 g of flour. This is 20% more than she needs.

How many grams of flour should Emma have weighed?

4 A full jar of salt weighs 750 g. One gram is about 0.035 oz.

What is the weight of the jar of salt to the nearest oz?

5 A box contains 8 jars of low calorie sweetener. Each jar weighs 35 g.

What is the weight of the 8 jars?

6 A packet of sugar weighs 2 kg.

What is the weight of the sugar in grams?

7  I am the sum of the multiples of 3 between 20 and 29. What am I?

Measures problems 3

1) Every second of every day 100 lightning bolts hit the ground somewhere in the world.

How many lightning bolts strike in 10 sec?

2) Meghan is making a skirt. She buys a length of material 0.58 m long. She cuts it into two equal lengths.

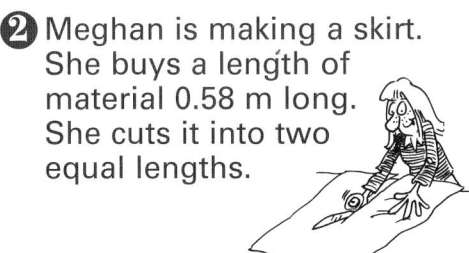

What is the length of each piece?

3) Eoghan buys a box of 10 table tennis balls. The box weighs 2.5 grams.

What is the weight of one ball?

4) Sam's dad buys a case of 10 bottles of wine that is on special offer at €35.99. Each bottle holds 700 mL of wine.

What is the total capacity of the 10 bottles in litres?

5) Andrew's room is cold in the winter. His mum buys two panel heaters. One is 63 cm × 95 cm, the other 50 cm × 75 cm.

What is the difference in area of both sides of the two heaters?

6) Alice finds that a golf ball weighs 0.043 kg and a tennis ball weighs 0.057 kg.

She puts both balls on the scales. What is the total weight of both balls in kg?

7)  I am the middle number of three consecutive numbers. The product of the three consecutive numbers is 17 550.

What am I?

Money problems 4

1) Mr and Mrs O'Keeffe book a cruise to Australia. It costs them €7479 each. They pay a deposit of €2500.

How much is left to pay?

2) A set of garden furniture normally costs €1190. In a sale it is reduced by 30%.

What is the price of the furniture in the sale?

3) Máire's dad has to go to France on business. He buys the case and the briefcase.

What is the total cost?

4) A theatre show has an afternoon and an evening performance every weekday.

On the first day the income from the two performances was €9457 and €12 818.

What was the total income for the day?

5) Daniel wants to learn to play an electric guitar. He buys one for €79.99. Later he sees the same guitar for sale in another shop for €82.50.

How much more was the guitar in the other shop?

6) The TV at Chris's house breaks. His dad buys both the TV and the DVD player.

Altogether how much does he pay?

7)

I am between 50 and 150.
I am 2 more than a multiple of 3.
I am 2 more than a multiple of 5.
I am 2 more than a multiple of 7.

What am I?

Number problems 11

1 In Brazil in 1990 the band A-Ha was watched by 195 000 people at a concert. In the same year 184 000 saw Paul McCartney in Brazil.

How many more watched A-Ha than Paul McCartney?

2 In Ancient Egypt Rames III built warships to defeat the Sea People. Each warship had 6 oars each side.

How many oars were needed for 40 warships?

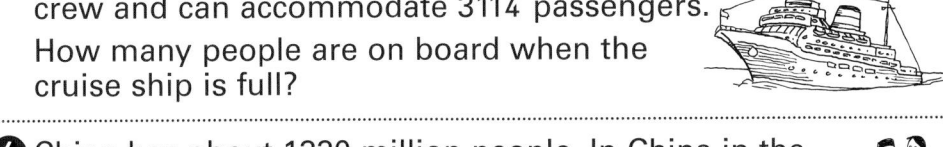

3 The cruise ship *Voyager of the Sea* has 1181 crew and can accommodate 3114 passengers.

How many people are on board when the cruise ship is full?

4 China has about 1330 million people. In China in the year 2000 there were 124.21 million children in primary schools and 53.84 million in secondary schools.

In 2001 how many children attended schools in China?

5 On average a human being takes 30 000 breaths in a day.

About how many breaths do you take in one hour?

6 In the year 2000 the population of the USA was 228.77 million. In Ireland it was 3.82 million.

In 2000, how many more people lived in the USA than in Ireland?

7

Add 2.5 to me and multiply the answer by 7. You will get 70.

What am I?

Number problems 12

1) In 1997 Heathrow airport had 44 262 000 passengers. London Gatwick had 19 417 000.

How many more passengers did Heathrow have than Gatwick?

2) Every second of every day 400 Kit-kats are eaten.

What is the total number of Kit-kats eaten in a day?

3) In Verkhoyansk, Siberia the temperature has been as high as 37°C and as low as –68°C.

What is the range of temperature?

4) In 1998 North Carolina, a state of the USA, had 7 425 183 people. Its neighbour South Carolina had 3 760 181.

How many more lived in North Carolina than in South Carolina?

5) In 1997 a total of 14 250 000 people visited Disneyland Paris.

On average how many people is this each day to the nearest whole number?

6) When completed in 1934 the Strahov Stadium in Prague held 240 000 spectators.

Wembley Stadium held only 30% as many.

How many people did Wembley hold?

7)  Divide me by 10 and subtract 3 from the answer. You will get 10.5.

What am I?

Number problems 13

❶ Ten minutes before the end of an Ireland v. New Zealand rugby match Ireland have 18 points and New Zealand have 13 points.

How many more points must New Zealand score to win the match?

❷ Caoimhe got 29 marks out of 50 in a maths test. The teacher re-marked her paper and this time she was awarded 62%.

How many extra marks did the teacher give Caoimhe when she re-marked the questions?

❸ A sheet has 5 stamps in each row and 10 in each column. At the start of a day a post office has 50 sheets of stamps. At the end of the day it has $10\frac{1}{2}$ sheets left.

How many stamps did it sell in the day?

❹ Mrs Evans orders 200 copies of a magazine to sell in her shop. The magazines come packed in twelves.

How many packs and how many separate copies will she get?

❺ Philip's mum and dad had a party. They bought 5 cases of wine with 6 bottles per case, 8 cartons of beer with 8 bottles per carton and 10 packs of juice with 10 bottles per pack.

How many bottles did they buy?

❻ Refuse collectors usually empty 600 dustbins every weekday. On a Monday it snowed and they only emptied one-quarter of this.

How many did they need to empty in the rest of the week to empty their weekly load?

❼  *Subtract me from 10 and add 0.7 to the answer. You will get 4.* What am I?

Review problems 4

1. The area of Whitelake Pleasure Park is 170 000 m². Of this area, 25% is covered by 150 rides, 35% is shops and cafes and 15% is theatres and cinemas. The rest is parkland and walkways. What area is parkland and walkways?

2. When did the Grand Derby celebrate its 50th Anniversary?

3. How many people are in the eight trains on the Grand Derby when they are all full?

4. Each train is 9.5 metres long. When a pair of trains in the Grand Derby stop at the station the four pairs are equi-distant on the track. What is the distance between the back of one pair of trains and the front of the next?

5. How many years after the Grand Derby was constructed was the Loopy Loop built?

6. What is the length of the track in the Loopy Loop that is not part of the vertical loop?

7. When the Loopy Loop has 11 adults and 5 children what is the total income?

8. Jamie buys 7 sticks of rock. Later he goes back for 3 more. How much would he have saved had he bought all ten sticks at the same time?

9. Mr Fitzpatrick buys a large baseball cap for himself and three animal face masks and five balloons for his children. Altogether how much does he pay?

10. How many metres higher is the Grand Derby than the Loopy Loop?

11. It is planned to build a Vertical Drop ride which will be 72 m. What fraction of the height of the Vertical Drop is an 8 metre lamp post?

12. In 1997 Disneyland Paris had 14 250 000 visitors. The Whitelake Pleasure Park had 1 389 000 visitors. How many more visitors did Disneyland Paris have than Whitelake Pleasure Park?

Number problems 14

1 A trailer can carry 72 bales of hay. A tractor pulls the full trailer nine times from the fields to the barn.

How many bales are taken to the barn?

2 At the start of the year a restaurant has 860 glasses. During the year 15% of the glasses are broken.

How many glasses are broken?

3 A container ship carries 4422 containers from Malaysia to Ireland and 3795 from Ireland to Australia.

What is the total number of containers the ship carries on the two journeys?

4 It is believed that there are 1537 volcanoes in the world. Some 569 of them are said to be active.

How many volcanoes are dormant (not active)?

5 In a hairdressing competition each of the seven judges award Julie 9.4 marks out of 10.

What is Julie's total score?

6 A machine makes 1 million chocolates every day. One day, on inspection, it is found that 10 000 of the chocolates are mis-shapen.

What percentage of the chocolates are mis-shapen?

7  *I am two decimal numbers. The sum of my numbers is 10. The difference between my numbers is 4.4.* What am I?

Money problems 5

1. Lucy sends a 120 g letter for €0.59 and a 310 g letter for €0.87.
What is the total cost of the two letters?

2. Christina sends 23 letters to New Zealand. Each letter weighs 430 g. The total cost is €72.22.
What is the value of the stamps on each letter?

3. Mrs Brady has an electrical shop. She orders eight electric irons at €31.95 each. Later she sells all the irons at €34.75 each.
What is the total profit Mrs Brady makes on the eight irons?

4. A post office has available 8c, 20c, 30c, 37c, 40c, 41c and 45c stamps. Jill buys four stamps to send a 500 g letter for €1.58.
Which four stamps does she buy?

5. A superstore has 37 Tardis computers in stock. It sells all of them.
What is the total income the shop gets from the sale?

6. The cost of a 7 day holiday in Trabolgan is €289 per adult and €176 per child. The total cost for the Foley family is €1571.
How many adults and children are in the Foley family?

7.  *I am a decimal number. Double me and add 3.4 to the answer. You will get 20.* What am I?

Number problems 15

1 Rob did a dive with a degree of difficulty of 8.7. He did a second dive that had a degree of difficulty double his first.

What is the degree of difficulty of the second dive?

2 In Sweden in 1995 there were 1 652 000 children aged 0 to 14 and 1 720 000 people aged 15 to 29.

Altogether how many were 29 or younger?

3 At a golf driving range each player is given four boxes of balls. One weekend 152 players visit the range.

Altogether how many balls are given to the 152 players?

4 In ten games a hockey team scores a total of 37 goals.

What is the average number of goals per game?

5 In 1900 the population of the world was 1633 million. By 1995 it had risen to 5734 million.

By how many had the population increased from 1900 to 1995?

6 One summer's day a boat on the River Shannon carried a total of 1218 passengers. On each trip it carried 87 passengers. How many trips did it make?

7  *I am a decimal number. Add 2.6 to me and double the answer. You will get 11.* What am I?

Number problems 16

1 For every person who lives in London there are 25 who live in Hong Kong. The population of London is 7.5 million.
What is the population of Hong Kong?

2 In 2000 Japan had 126 million people. The population in China was ten times this.

How many people lived in China in the year 2000?

3 The population of Sweden in the year 2000 was 9 million. Eight per cent of the people are over 75 years old.

How many people are 75 or younger?

4 An aircraft has one cabin attendant for every 40 passengers. A jumbo jet has 560 passengers.
How many cabin attendants will it have?

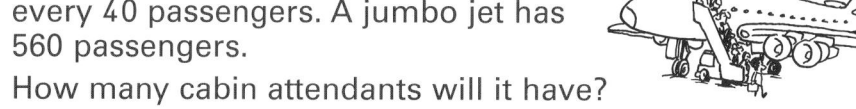

5 Every day France has 180 000 foreign visitors. This is ten times the number that visit Ireland.

How many foreign visitors does Ireland have every day?

6 Debbie was given the same score on the parallel bars and the horse. Her total for the two events was 17.4.

What was her score on the parallel bars?

7 *I am half-way between 3.9 and 8.5.* What am I?

Number problems 17

1) On a course at Delphi Adventure Centre there are 58 boys and 45 girls.
How many children are on the course?

2) Of all the recordings sold in 2000, 2 in every 3 were CDs. In Ireland 810 000 recordings were sold.
How many were CDs?

3) A car-carrying ship is loaded with 12 different models of car. There are 100 of each model.
How many cars are on the ship?

4) On a three-masted schooner there are 42 children on a training holiday. Of these, 17 are girls.
How many are boys?

5) An Airbus carries a total of 350 passengers. Of these, 90% travel in Economy Class.

How many are in Economy Class?

6) There are 28 million golfers in the world. One-hundredth of them play in Scotland.

How many golfers play in Scotland?

7)  *I am a prime number. The sum of my two digits is 14.* What am I?

Number problems 18

1 The *Tír na nÓg* has 522 outside cabins and 189 inside cabins. What is the total number of cabins on the ship?

2 When full there are 2385 passengers and crew on board. There are half as many crew as passengers. How many crew are there?

3 Since its maiden voyage the *Tír na nÓg* has made 1000 voyages carrying a total of 1.42 million passengers.
On average how many passengers did it carry on each voyage?

4 On a cruise to the Mediterranean there were 1590 passengers. The restaurant had two sittings for the evening meal and the number of passengers was divided equally between the two. How many passengers were at each sitting?

5 Before the start of a cruise 1000 boxes of wine are taken on board. Each box holds 12 bottles, each bottle holding 700 mL of wine. How many bottles of wine are taken on board?

6 At one port of call the *Tír na nÓg* has to anchor in the harbour. The passengers are taken ashore in small boats. Each small boat holds 70 people.
How many journeys from the ship to shore are needed to carry all the 1594 passengers who wish to go ashore?

7  *I am the difference between two square numbers. The sum of the two square numbers is 85.* What am I?

Review problems 5

1. How many schools are taking part in the swimming gala?
2. The width of the pool is 10.5 metres. The lanes are of equal width. What is the width of a lane?
3. The pool is 25 m long and slopes evenly from the shallow to the deep end. What is the depth of the water half-way along the length of the pool?
4. How many lengths of the pool did P. Burke swim to win his race?
5. The pool has 315 000 litres of water. It takes 4 hr 22 min to fill the pool. What is the average number of litres pumped into the pool each second to the nearest whole number?
6. Which school is winning the competition?
7. How many points is Clonakilty behind Scoil Naomh Eoin?
8. In each event the winner gets 6 points, the second 5 points, and so on, to the last swimmer who gets 1 point. How many points did M. Byrne get in the Boys' 100 m Freestyle?
9. How many events have been shown on the score board?
10. The result of the Boys' 100 m Freestyle has not yet been entered on the Points Board. Write what the new points will look like when it has been entered.
11. How many seconds longer than one minute did W. Lynch take to complete the Boys' 100 m Freestyle?
12. By how many seconds did P. Burke win the Boys' 100 m Freestyle?
13. There were 376 people watching the Gala. There was no charge for watching, but every spectator contributed 10c to charity. What is the total amount collected for charity?
14. Seventy-five per cent of the 376 watching are children. How many adults are watching?
15. There were 20 individual races. No child was allowed to compete in more than one individual race. How many children took part in the races?

Capacity problems 1

1. Jake buys a goldfish. It is 16 cm long of which 3.5 cm is tail. Jake is advised to put 4 litres of water into the tank for every 5 cm length of his fish less the length of its tail.

How many litres of water should Jake put in the tank?

2. A oil depot has ten storage tanks. Each tank holds 1.5 million litres of oil.

What is the total capacity of the ten tanks?

3. A one litre bottle of apple drink contains 30% pure juice.

How many millilitres of pure juice are in one bottle?

4. Jill's mum fills her car with 10 litres of petrol.

How many mL is 10 litres?

5. Every week the Keogh family has a total of 10 baths. They use a total of 175 litres in the week.

On average how many litres are used for each bath?

6. Sam uses concentrated orange juice to make a drink. He uses the instructions to make 250 mL.

High juice
Dilute 1 part with 4 parts water

How many millilitres of water does he use?

7.  *I am the difference between the smallest and the largest two-digit prime numbers.* What am I?

Measures problems 4

1 A new straight road is 100 m in length. Kerbstones, 92 cm long, are placed each side of the road.
How many whole kerbstones are needed?

2 On 14th September 1987 the *New York Times* newspaper had 1612 pages. It weighed a total of 5.4 kg.
How much did each sheet weigh to the nearest tenth of a gram? (Remember there are 4 pages to a sheet.)

3 Pepi II became Pharoah of Egypt in 2246 BC when he was 6 years old. He died at the age of 102.
In what year did he die?

4 The river Amazon, in South America, is 6448 km long. The river Nile, in Egypt, is 232 km longer than the Amazon.
What is the length of the Nile?

5 Rachel has a cup that holds 284 mL and a tablespoon that holds 18 mL.
How many tablespoonfuls would she need to fill the cup?

6 The Caspian Sea, the world's largest lake, is 371 000 sq km in area. The world's second largest lake is Lake Superior which is 82 414 sq km.
How many sq km larger is the Caspian Sea than Lake Superior?

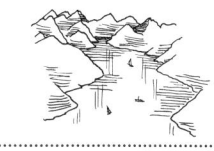

7  *I am a square number. Both of my digits are even.* What am I?

Number problems 19

1) In the 1996 Olympic Games in Atlanta, USA there were 10 310 competitors. This was 4225 more than the Montreal Games in Canada 30 years earlier.

How many competitors were in the Montreal Olympics?

2) In 2000 New Zealand had 3.3 million English speakers. Australia had five times as many as New Zealand.

How many English speakers did Australia have in the year 2000?

3) An actor playing Hamlet in the Shakespeare play *Hamlet* has 1422 lines to memorise.

How many lines would an actor playing Hamlet have said after 1000 performances?

4) Up to the 1996 Olympic Games the UK had won 395 gold, 215.5 silver and 213 bronze medals.

What is the total number of medals won by the UK?

5) In the 1950 soccer World Cup game between Brazil and Spain there were 152 772 spectators. This was 47 082 fewer than watched Brazil play Uruguay.

How many watched Brazil play Uruguay?

6) In the year 2000 the population of France was 59 million. There are 1433 radios per 1000 people.

How many radios were there in France in the year 2000?

7)  *I am the square of a prime number. The sum of my three digits is 10.* What am I?

Money problems 6

1 Rachel's mum books a holiday for both of them at Torquay. The cost of the holiday is €299 for her mum and €159 for her.

What is the total cost of the holiday?

2 The normal price of a Saxon car is €8995. In a sale Mr Collins saves €1365.

What is the percentage saving he made to the nearest whole number?

3 Mrs Brook went on a cruise to Alaska to see whales, dolphins and glaciers. The cruise cost her €2598 and the executive flight to Vancouver cost €1659.

What was the total cost?

4 Mr and Mrs Sheehan took their five children and four more children to see the play *Visiting Grandma*. A child's ticket cost €4.75 and an adult's ticket was twice this.

What did it cost Mr and Mrs Sheehan?

5 Jennifer saw a digital TV and a DVD player for sale at 'Buy Here' for a total of €1390. Later she saw the same items for sale at 'Rocket TV' for €1199.99

How much cheaper were the items at 'Rocket TV' than at 'Buy Here'?

6 The cost of a wildlife safari holiday is €1398 in January and €1882 in December.

How much less is it in January than in December?

7  I am the difference between two square numbers. The two square numbers are between 550 and 650.

What am I?

Number problems 20

1 The island of Cyprus has a population of 650 000. Of these, 78% are Greek Cypriots and 18% are Turkish Cypriots.
How many are Greek Cypriots and how many are Turkish Cypriots?

2 In the year 2000 the *Sun* newspaper sold 3 767 941 copies while the *Mirror* sold 2 321 608.
How many more copies did the *Sun* sell than the *Mirror*?

3 The estimated population of China for the year 2000 was 1 253 438 000. About one-half of them are females.

What was the estimate of females in China in the year 2000?

4 In the year 2000 in Russia 7 849 000 children went to primary school and 13 732 000 went to secondary school.

What was the total number of children who went to school in 2000?

5 The number of people in Jamaica is 2.7 million. The number is growing at 2% per annum.

How many people will be living in Jamaica in one year's time?

6 In a gymnastics competition Marie was awarded 8.3 points by each of two judges and 7.9 by each of three judges.

What was the total score awarded by the five judges?

7  *I am the sum of four consecutive prime numbers. I am between 125 and 140.* What am I?

Number problems 21

1. In the league Robert scored 4 goals and 17 points. In the Championship he scored 2 goals and 22 points. If 3 points is the equivalent of 1 goal, what was Robert's total score for the season when converted to goals?

2. A block of flats has 315 windows. In a storm 159 of them are broken. The next day workers manage to repair 38 of the windows.

   How many windows are unbroken after the repairs?

3. In a tube there are 84 sweets. There are an equal number of seven different colours of sweet. Aoife eats five of the red ones.
   How many red sweets are left?

4. Five carrying cages each with ten parrots arrived on a plane at Dublin Airport. The Animal Welfare Officer removed the parrots and put them six to a cage.
   How many cages did she need?

5. A shopkeeper got 30 books of 12 stamps from the post office. In one week he sells 272 of the stamps.

   How many full books and separate stamps has he left?

6. A DIY store had 19 tins of white paint on the shelves. It received a delivery of 50 more tins. All the tins were displayed equally on three shelves.
   How many tins of paint were on each shelf?

7. Add 3 to me and halve the answer. The number you will get has six factors, four of which are 2, 4, 7 and 14. What am I?

Review problems 6

1) As sound travels more slowly than light we hear thunder 3 seconds later than we see the lightning for every kilometre distance we are away from the centre of the storm.
How far are we away from a storm when thunder is heard 1 minute later than the lightning is seen?

2) The Indian Ocean is 10 000 km across at its widest point. It is getting 20 cm wider every year.

How many years will it be before it is 10 001 km across?

3) The weight of an average African elephant is 6300 kg. The blocks of stone used to build the pyramids were two and a half times the weight of an average African elephant.
What was the weight of a block?

4) Every 100 metres up a mountain the temperature drops 0.6°C. Mt Everest is 8850 m above sea level.
If the temperature at sea level is 32°C what is the temperature at the summit of Mt Everest?

5) A bottle holds 100 mL of cough medicine.

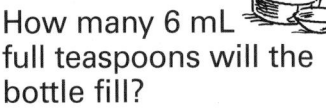

How many 6 mL full teaspoons will the bottle fill?

6) The surface area of the Earth is 510.07 million km². Rainforests cover about one-tenth of the Earth's surface.

What is the approximate area of rainforest?

7) The cash price of the car is €5995.
How much more does it cost when making a deposit of €99 and 60 monthly payments of €127.66?